# HAWAII
## THE ALOHA STATE

By Allan Seiden

*An outrigger canoe in the multi-hued waters off Waikiki.*

# Paradise of the Pacific

All the visions that stir the imagination when the tropics come to mind are to be found in Hawaii. The glistening waters off a sun drenched beach, lush green mountains laced with waterfalls, the romantic reverie of palms silhouetted against a vibrant dusk sky, and moonlit nights caressed by gentle trade winds are but some of the ways in which Hawaii epitomizes paradise.

Hawaii was admitted as the 50th State on August 21, 1959, having been administered as an American territory since 1898. For five years before that it had been a republic under the control of American planters and businessmen who had helped overthrow the monarchy and the rule of Queen Liliuokalani.

It is believed that the earliest inhabitants of the Islands were Polynesians who over a span of centuries had come from southeast Asia by way of the Marquesas and the Society Islands. In time contact was lost with these home islands and Hawaii developed its own distinctive Polynesian culture. A feudalistic lifestyle emerged, with the ruling alii (nobility) and kahunas (priests) controlling a population of farmers, fishermen, warriors and slaves. The kapu system was tied closely to their religion and consisted of rules and regulations that insured the rule of the alii and kahunas.

It was Captain James Cook's arrival in 1778 that introduced the archipelago he called the Sandwich Islands to the western world. At the time of Cook's arrival Hawaii was in the midst of interisland wars being waged by chiefs trying to extend their dominions. By 1810, with the aid of foreign advisors and modern weaponry, Kamehameha I, the greatest of the Hawaiian chiefs, had united the islands into a single kingdom.

By the time the first missionaries arrived from New England in 1820, foreign influence had already played a role in causing the abolition of the kapu system and the destruction of the gods and temples of the old religion. The missionaries played a vital role in this transitional period, not only introducing Christianity to the Hawaiians with the support of the royal family and alii, but also creating an alphabet for the unwritten Hawaiian language, establishing schools where science, history and technology were taught, developing modern agricultural techniques, and coordinating the establishment of nineteenth century American-style democracy as advisors to Hawaii's kings.

Westernization brought with it the end of the feudal land-owning system, and in the mid-nineteenth century the lands were divided between the crown, the alii, and the commoners. This change helped pave the way for plantation agriculture, which prospered with the introduction of sugar and later pineapple.

Sugar was to trigger further changes, for with Hawaii's native population dying off from a combination of introduced diseases and spiritual demoralization, new sources of labor meant the importation of foreigners. Decade to decade the source of contract labor changed, drawing Chinese, Japanese, American, Puerto Rican, Portuguese, Korean and Filipino immigrants to Hawaii's shores, thus remaking the genetic landscape.

Despite growth and change, Hawaii remains a place for indulging in romantic imagery. These unique islands are a place of marvelous contrasts where Polynesia, America and the Orient converge in a setting of unexcelled beauty.

Aloha . . . it is easy to understand why it is the most universally known word of the Hawaiian language. It is used in greetings of hello, goodbye and love. To take its message seriously and live out its meaning often is to carry the spirit of Hawaii with you wherever you go.

# Oahu

## THE GATHERING PLACE

Oahu once served as a meeting place for Hawaii's island chiefs, and so it is called "the gathering place." Today this third largest island of the Hawaiian chain is home to three-quarters of Hawaii's more than one million people. The city of Honolulu, with a population inching toward 400,000, serves as the economic, social, and political capital of Hawaii. Waikiki, Honolulu's beachfront resort, is about four miles from downtown. Highrise hotels line Waikiki Beach, hosting millions of visitors a year from around the world with an array of shops, restaurants, and activities.

Another Oahu awaits those who go beyond urban Honolulu. It's an island of dramatically eroded cliffs that fall to multi-hued seas, of long stretches of undeveloped beach, of lush tropical rainforest and vast fields of sugarcane and pineapple. An island formed by the merging lava of two great volcanoes . . . the Koolau, whose mountains overlook Honolulu and Waikiki, and the Waianae, which looms in the distance. Extinct for countless centuries, time and erosion have sculpted them into a series of giant palis (cliffs), magnificent bays (including Pearl Harbor), and meandering beaches. All this and more are Oahu, today as in ancient times, "the gathering place" of Hawaii.

*W*orld famous Waikiki Beach with volcanic Diamond Head Crater.

*W*aikiki's shops offer everything from native souvenirs to designer label apparel, from coral and jade jewelry to expensive original art.  right

*Night falls on Kalakaua Avenue, Waikiki's main thoroughfare.*

**D**iamond Head Crater from the air. *above*

**W**indsurfing at dusk off Diamond Head. *left*

**H**ilton Hawaiian Village and its beach-lined lagoon. *right*

*D*ancers perform at the Kodak Hula Show in Kapiolani Park. *left*

*D*iamond Head serves as a backdrop for a giraffe and her newborn at the Honolulu Zoo. *right*

*T*he lyrically named humuhu-munukunukuapuaa, Hawaii's State Fish, can be viewed at the Waikiki Aquarium. Both the aquarium and the zoo are in Kapiolani Park. *below*

*F*eeding time in the Reef
Tank at Sea Life Park.    above

*P*layful porpoises showing off
at Sea Life Park.  left

*P*ink flamingos are one of the
many attractions at Paradise
Park.  above right

*H*ang gliding over Makapuu Beach and Rabbit Island. Makapuu is famous for body surfing.  above

*H*anauma Bay, a volcanic crater that has eroded and been flooded by the sea, provides excellent snorkeling opportunities in its reef-sheltered waters.  right

*T*he Blow Hole near Koko Head. The sea is forced through a small hole in the lava ledge and blows sea spray high into the air.  below

*T*he Mormon Temple at Laie is part of thousands of acres of Church owned lands along Oahu's North Shore.  above

*E*ntertainment at the Polynesian Cultural Center includes a daily canoe pageant and a nightly extravaganza on the outdoor stage of the center's theater.  left

*W*indward Oahu is revealed in a dramatic panorama from the Nuuanu Pali Lookout. below

*The hibiscus, Hawaii's state flower, blooms in a wide variety of shapes and colors.*

*Waimea Falls Park provides a tropical setting for a swim.*
below

*W*aimea Beach Park, one of the North Shore's beautiful beaches. Winter waves make it popular with surfers.  left

*S*urfing the North Shore's winter waves.  below

*T*he volcanic soils of the Schofield Plains nurtures a rich harvest of pineapples. *above*

*A* ripe pineapple ready for harvest. *left*

*T*he design of the Hawaii State Capitol symbolizes the volcanic origins of the islands.  above.

*A*loha Tower, built in 1926, was for many years Hawaii's tallest building. The Tower's tenth floor balconies offer panoramic views from the mountains to the sea, from downtown to Diamond Head.  right

*The USS Arizona Memorial rises above the hulk of the battleship aboard which 1,102 servicemen lost their lives during the attack on Pearl Harbor, December 7, 1941. right*

*The Punchbowl National Memorial Cemetery of the Pacific is the final resting place of more than 25,000 American servicemen and women. In Hawaiian it is called Puowaina, "Hill of Sacrifice." below*

*T*he statue of Kamehameha the Great stands in front of the historic Judiciary Building. Each year on June 11, the greatest of Hawaii's kings is honored with a parade before which his statue is draped in flower leis, some as long as 40 feet. *left*

*I*olani Palace, completed in 1882 during the reign of King David Kalakaua, has been fully restored. It is the only royal palace in the United States. *above*

*G*azebo on Iolani Palace grounds. *right*

***D**usk falls at Kapalua with a silhouette of Molokai in the background.*

***A** majestic waterfall flows in the Kipahulu Valley.  right*

# Maui

## THE VALLEY ISLAND

Maui No Ka Oi, Maui is the Best. This phrase is used by residents and visitors alike to describe this beautiful island. Second largest of the Hawaiian chain, the centrally located Maui town of Lahaina served as Hawaii's capital for the first decades of the nineteenth century, after which it emerged as a primary mid-Pacific port of call for hundreds of reprovisioning whaling and trade ships each year. The tens of thousands of acres planted in sugarcane and pineapple tell of the century that followed with plantation agriculture as king.

Today Maui plays host to visitors drawn by the awesome beauty of Haleakala National Park, Hana's glorious tropical rainforest with its waterfalls and natural pools, and a coastal string of beaches and resorts that offer every sort of vacation option. For many it's the best of all possible worlds, the perfect blend of the old Hawaii and the new.

*I*ao Needle rises 1,200 feet
from the floor of an often
cloud-draped ravine in the
heart of the West Maui
Mountains.  left

*T*he Seven Pools, fed by a
series of waterfalls, are
located in a coastal portion
of Haleakala National Park
near Hana.   above

*The* head of a giant humpback whale rises above the water's surface off the Lahaina coast. During the nineteenth century, Lahaina was the "whaling capital of the world."  *left*

*P*icturesque Lahaina Harbor and the historic Pioneer Inn. *above*

*A*n aerial view of Lahaina, surrounding canefields and the dramatic West Maui Mountains.  *left*

*T*he narrow gauge track of the Lahaina, Kaanapali & Pacific Railroads carries visitors on trains like those used in harvesting Maui's canefields at the turn of the century. *below*

*Haleakala, whose summit encloses the world's largest dormant volcanic crater, is 7½ miles long, 2½ miles wide, and nearly 3,000 feet deep. Its floor includes a magnificent array of colorful cinder cones, 400–1,000 feet high.*

**K**aanapali's south beach from Black Rock.  *above*

**R**emote Hana lies nestled between the large bay from which it takes its name and the pastures of the Hana Ranch.  *right*

**S**unbathers enjoy the beaches that line the coast from Maalaea to Kihei, and Wailea to Makena.  *left*

*Sunset silhouettes a surfer at Bali Hai. Within a mile of this beach the road ends at the base of the magnificent Na Pali Cliffs.*

*A rainbow forms over lush*

# Kauai

## THE GARDEN ISLAND

Easternmost and oldest of the major Hawaiian Islands, lushly tropical Kauai is Hawaii at its most romantic. Verdant growth, magnificent gardens, plummeting waterfalls that veil thousand foot cliffs clothed in fern and forest support Kauai's nickname, "the garden isle."

Nature showed no restraint in creating Kauai, carving great canyons, valleys, mountains and sea cliffs from the long extinct volcano called Waialeale. Today Waialeale's usually cloud-banked summit is considered the wettest spot on earth, averaging between 450-650 inches annually.

But much of Kauai's beach-lined coast is clear of this upcountry rain zone, providing visitors with settings made legendary in films ranging from South Pacific to the remake of King Kong. For the distinctive beauty of the south seas, no place in Hawaii outdoes Kauai.

*A* helicopter tour skirts the cliffs and valleys of the inaccessible Na Pali Coast. *above*

*W*aimea Canyon winds 10 miles from Kauai's interior to the sea. The 2,857-foot gorge, carved into the Kokee Plateau by the Waimea River, presents an ever-changing color scheme that ranges from the soft greens and blues of the morning to the vibrant coppers and reds of late afternoon. *right*

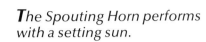*T*he Spouting Horn performs
with a setting sun.

*C*rescent beaches and tropic
seas make sunny Poipu one
of Kauai's most popular resort
areas.  *below*

*Hanalei Valley's taro fields provide a breeding ground for a number of rare Hawaiian birds. above*

*Lovely Wailua Falls. left*

*Visitors are serenaded while inside the Fern Grotto. right*

**P**rinceville benefits from what
may be the most spectacular
resort setting in Hawaii. In the
distance, Hanalei Bay and the
road to the Na Pali Coast.
above

**L**umahai is one of Hawaii's
most beautiful beaches. It
was here that portions of
South Pacific were filmed.
right

# Molokai Lanai

Until about 50 years ago, Molokai was known as the "lonely island" because sufferers of leprosy were segregated by the natural isolation of the Kalaupapa Peninsula. Today Kalaupapa attracts visitors as a National Historical Park. Molokai's off-the-beaten-path country feel and the mountainous scenery of its justly acclaimed North Coast are other highlights of a Molokai visit. Today pasture covers thousands of acres, including many of those once planted in pineapple.

Pineapple is still grown in abundance on neighboring Lanai. Smallest of Hawaii's main islands, Lanai takes its nickname, the Pineapple Island, from this tropical fruit. Just about all of Lanai's 2,400 people live in the plantation town of Lanai City. Lanai invites the adventurous to set out and explore its upcountry forests and isolated beaches, or enjoy snorkeling and scuba in some of Hawaii's clearest waters.

*The north coast of Molokai is one of the most spectacular in Hawaii.*

*Lying at the base of Molokai's north coast cliffs, the Kalaupapa Peninsula was selected as the site for Hawaii's first leper colony because of its isolation. Though it still has a resident community, Kalaupapa is now administered by the National Parks Service. left*

*Snorkelers prepare for a morning in waters off Hulopoe Beach, Lanai. right*

*Kilauea Volcano sends a fiery burst of lava and gas into the air. Kilauea and Mauna Loa, are among the most active volcanoes in the world. Both are located within the borders of Hawaii Volcanoes National Park, providing visitors with a chance to safely view one of nature's most awesome spectacles.*

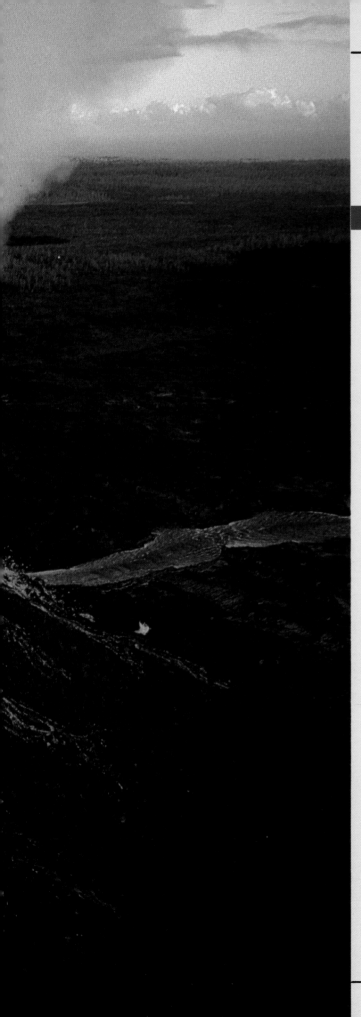

# Hawaii

## THE BIG ISLAND

More than twice as big as all the other islands combined, Hawaii, namesake of the archipelago, is an island of volcanic drama, great natural diversity and powerful links to the Polynesian past. Most heavily populated of the islands in ancient times, the Big Island's rebuilt heiaus (temples) today provide unique insights into the Hawaii of myth and legend.

The Big Island provides insights into other mysteries as well. Its two active volcanoes, Kilauea and Mauna Loa, both contained within Hawaii Volcanoes National Park, are among the safest and most active volcanoes in the world.

History and volcanic fireworks are a prelude to the Big Island's exciting diversity. Also to be found are upcountry ranches that raise thousands of head of cattle; orchid, plumeria and anthurium nurseries that produce millions of saleable flowers; active sugar plantations, macadamia nut orchards and coffee farms; dramatically eroded valleys and towering sea cliffs; and a range of top quality resorts from which to set out and explore. All told, it's a combination that makes the Big Island impressive in more than just size.

*From December through May, snow often accumulates on the high altitude slopes of Mauna Kea and Mauna Loa, allowing great skiing under the tropical sun.*

*Kilauea Volcano explodes with a fiery burst of lava and gas.*

*H*ilo's Rainbow Falls, according to Hawaiian legend, is the birthplace of rainbows.  *above*

*K*ealakekua Bay, on the South Kona Coast, offers excellent snorkeling opportunities. A monument marks the spot where Captain James Cook lost his life in a conflict with the native Hawaiians in 1779.  *above right*

*A* giant marlin is weighed in at Kailua Kona Harbor. The Big Island's west coast offers some of the best sport fishing in the world.  *far right*

*T*he sea wall at Kailua-Kona with Hulihee Palace and the steeple of Mokuaikaua Church, reminders of Kona's nineteenth century charm. Hawaiian royalty used Hulihee as a summer home.  *right*

*L*ava ash was responsible for
the formation of the Kalapana
Black Sand Beach.  *left*

*T*he Parker Ranch in upcountry
Kamuela.  *above*

*A*naehoomalu, one of the
resort beaches along the
Kohala Coast.   above

*K*ona's Magic Sand Beach is
also known as Disappearing
Sands since it is often washed
away by the heavy winter
surf.   left

*S*unset at Puuhonua O'Honaunau. In ancient times this place of refuge was a sanctuary for law-breakers, defeated warriors and non-combatants when tribal battles raged. Once purified by a temple priest, those who had reached the Puuhonua could go free without fear of reprisal.